How to Recruit Doctors into your MLM or Network Marketing Team

by showing them a NO Warm Market System

David Williams

How to Recruit Doctors into your MLM or Network Marketing Team

Best Selling Author of:

The Simplest, Shortest, Most Powerful MLM and Network Marketing Prospect Control and Closing Lines and Scripts

You can find it on Amazon Kindle.

ISBN 978-1484121986

Table of Contents

Introduction

What this book will teach you:

How to Recruit Doctors – including scripts

Where to Find Doctors – It's not where you think

A new source of Doctors (medical) who are not busy

It's...

Perfect for the Wellness Industry

Not buying Leads

Not working the phone

Having a Doctor in your MLM or Network Marketing team can be very profitable if you follow the system revealed in this book. If you have bought into the idea that Doctors are hard to recruit or difficult to work with, forget those thoughts; this book is going to teach you an amazing system to recruit Doctors and an amazing system for you to build a huge, profitable and unstoppable leg under them - without the Doctor using any of their warm market, 'buying leads' or touching the phone!

Full Discloser: This is a short book. It's less than 50 pages long. It contains no fluff or padding. It's direct and to the point. The system contained is worth hundreds of thousands of dollars in sales, and could retire you. Really. Forget the low price, forget the number of pages. This book will show you a fool proof system that ANY one can follow to build an unstoppable MLM Network Marketing business by recruiting Doctors. I have made it newbie friendly, but those with experience will take this system and put into practice very quickly.

NOTE: This system assumes you are in a nutrition or health type business. If you are selling something very different, this book will give you a few ideas, but you will have to adapt it. If you are in the Wellness industry, this book is a treasure map and it's ready to show you the way.

What's in it?

This book will cover, step by step, and in very detailed and specific language:

How to recruit Doctors

The 'invisible' secret source of Doctors without a practice that are begging for something like what you will be able to show them

How to recruit busy Doctors with a practice and who have zero time

How to avoid the 'I don't want to go to my contacts/warm market' objection because you will be teaching them a system that requires ZERO warm market

No 'buying leads'

How to fill, yes FILL, meeting rooms with prospects all eager to join and try your products

NO conference calls, webinars, websites, Fanpages, autoresponders etc.

This is the full system, from the free ads you will place to the words on the marketing material you will print. This approached is very inexpensive to follow, quick and easy to implement, and very straight forward.

Also included are the phone scripts and person to person scripts you need to use when speaking to the Doctors, their receptionists, and to use in getting the appointment.

Forget all the 'usual suspects' techniques, this is not about dropping off DVDs, inviting Doctors to conference calls, or creating special 'Doctors only' presentations. Forget all of that, and forget all of your old scripts and ads.

This system works for Doctors and requires NO Warm Market – I know I said that above, but it's very important you forget about their warm market.

You don't need any paid advertising, Facebook, Internet, Twitter etc., this is all offline, local, and affordable.

No one has taught you this before. Guaranteed.

***

In my experience, most Doctors don't succeed in MLM or Network Marketing because they are told to go after their warm market, their patients, or to 'buy leads and become a telemarketer'. Really? Really? Really?

No kidding they won't do it.

Now, this method for Doctors to create YOU a fortune in MLM will appeal to them. It involves no warm market, and no one-on-ones (time consuming for those with a busy practice), and can be done in the evenings or weekends. Its brilliant and it works. It's a goldmine for the Doctor, and for you who recruited him or her.

I'm going to show you where to get Doctors and how to approach them. I divide Doctors into two kinds, the busy types with a practice, and a second kind of medical Doctor you don't know about. This book will reveal to you a hidden world of Doctors who are not busy. I am going to share with you this source, give you all the scripts, the ads, the marketing materials, right down to what to say in the low cost marketing material for the system.

Nothing is left to chance.

Once again - Full Discloser: This is a small book – its contains no fluff. Its written to you as if I was speaking to you, and is not going to be a grammar teachers best seller. It's direct information that you can act on right away and is worth hundreds of thousands of dollars to you if do. It's less than 50 pages, but there is no padding.

However, I guarantee you don't have the knowledge or the system in this book, and were never taught it in any meeting, conference call or training. Your upline does not know about it, and the very few in the world who know about this system DON'T WANT ANYONE TO KNOW IT EITHER. Why? Because its making them a goldmine and they don't want this exposed.

Can you do it? YES, YES and YES.

First, I have made it simple and given you the full deal, the system, the things to say, the opening scripts, the follow up scripts, the ads and other marketing material. And this is gold. So YES, there is no reason that you can't follow this system. Even if you add only one Doctor to your team with this method, you will have a leg earning you $10,000 per month, or more, depending on your company's compensation plan. If you are in a Binary, it's pretty easy, get a Doctor on each side, and you can retire with a nice income. Keep adding more centers, and earn even more money. If you are in a stair step plan, you know the drill. This leg will be up and running on its own within 90 days, and you can be building another with the same system all over again.   If you are in some other pay plan, it works just as well.

If you don't take action, nothing will happen.

If someone does not work, nothing happens.   So, the caveat is getting a Doctor on your team who works smart – and the way to do that is to show him or her this system because it is tailor made for them.

Note well: this system NOT for non-Doctors (however it could be adapted for other Wellness professionals).

Why does this work?

Look, any Doctor who works hard in any network marketing company has an edge.   All over the world most of us are brought up to listen with respect to anyone with the word 'Doctor' in front of their name, it adds instant credibility. So, it's an advantage that can't be denied. This system will take that fact and turn it into gold.

Chapter 1 Busy 'normal' Doctors – by 'normal' I mean these are the type of Doctors we think of when we are told someone is a 'Doctor'. They are medical, working with a practice or in a hospital, always busy, and the last person you would approach about your business opportunity unless you have the self-confidence of King Kong.

Why are we afraid to approach a 'Doctor'? Because we assume that they are so involved with their profession/practice that they don't have the time or the energy to even look at something else. This is exactly why it's worth approaching them. I know, that sounds like such 'typical MLM upline' advice, but it's not, hear me out.

If you know a Doctor, say in his or her forties, chances are they are very busy, suffering from stress and burn-out and not enjoying the quality of life they can afford. Their job is no longer fun.

Consider this: they chose to be a Doctor when they were 17 or 18 years old, or even younger, when they had an idealized notion of what life as a Doctor would be like. Mostly this came from TV shows and not from reality.

The sad fact is life is not like a television show. It's not exciting, dramatic, fun or has a happy ending each episode. The problem faced by these Doctors is the fact that they don't really know anything else to do to replace the level of income they get and need, (children, university fees, mortgages, cars, etc.). They are often desperately unhappy, even to the point of self-medicating. They are desperate to make money OUTSIDE of their medical practice. This is why stock brokers do so well selling to Doctors, as Doctors really don't know anything outside their practice, and will typically buy into many bad investment deals because they are taught to trust specialists.

This is why you do NEED to approach these people, but you need to do it with someone in your upline who is successful and will be able to be the 'specialist'. Don't try and do it yourself if you are a newbie. If you do know what you are doing, and you are at least mid-level in your company's marketing structure, sponsored a few people and don't need hand holding, you can do this on your own. If that is the case, you are the specialist.

Script For newbie's working with their upline:

Using the web, search for Doctors in your LOCAL area. You will know why I say 'local area' by the time you have read this book. Call them up, or leave a message for them to call regarding a business concept. When they call, you act only as the broker, you have to get them together with your upline (use their name, don't say upline), 'who is a specialist at making money with natural health products in the main stream market, and there could be a place for someone like you who had a medical background, in a passive or active way, I don't have time to discuss it now, but when could I get you two together? This specialist is in town for the next 5 days, and we could do a lunch, breakfast or meet later after your day is over? When can I set this up for you two? I think it could be a great fit.' If you only get the receptionist, use the same script, it will get you a call back from the Doctor, or an appointment very quickly.

If you are experienced use this script:

I'm a marketing specialist currently working with natural health products in the main stream market, and there could be a place for someone like you who has a medical background, in a passive or active way, to be part of our promotional campaign. I don't want to go over the details over the phone as I'm about to head into a meeting, however if you/or the Doctor is interesting in diversifying their income flow, I'd like to get together. When could we meet? When can you set this up for us? I think you could be a great fit.'

If pushed for some more details, say this, 'I'm in events, and seminar productions, and this product is being introduced to the market through some events that I am setting up, but, for more details, I'm afraid we must meet'.

Don't say anything else or answer any other questions, use time as a reason, YOU are busy, and chances are they are too. Your upline specialist will take it from there.

How to Recruit more Doctors by visiting them:

Go to Doctor's offices:

Knock on doors in areas where there are lots of Doctors' offices, often this is near hospitals. Be sure you are in a business suit, (tie for men, business dress for women – NOT business casual). Go in early in the morning, start at 8AM. Carry a brief case, you want to look like a pharmaceutical sales person.

You'll see a receptionist:

'Hi, how are you doing, (wait or go on), I'm David Williams and I just wanted to ask the Doctor some questions, does he/she have a minute?'

If they are busy, you need to have a question for the receptionist, this will depend on your product industry, but this script can be easily adapted:

"Look, I am just wondering if the Doctor would be interested in talking to me about leading some seminars in the mainstream nutrition area /fitness arena" – or something that is vague, but conjures up lots of interesting questions, but is too confusing for the receptionist to answer, forcing her to get the Doctor or for you to be allowed in to see the Doctor. This bears repeating, your statement must sound intelligent, but must be something that you know the receptionist will not understand, or be willing to say 'NO' to you. That is your only goal with the receptionist, DO NOT GIVE THEM ANY INFORMATION or have any company brochures visible. Don't wear a button with your company logo, a pin with your rank, or wear anything that makes you look like you are in an MLM. You don't want them to make any preconceived notions.

You need to think out of the box for finding a few words that sound interesting, intriguing, and force the person to get their boss as they don't know what you really mean, but it could be important.

Here is another example of what I doing this, albeit a little different, used in a classified ad.

Years ago, I consulted with some NSA distributors. This was in the days before Juice Plus, when NSA only sold water filters. NSA was so well known, that all the ads for other MLM opportunities would say '...this is NOT water filters' so even if you did not know about NSA or water filters, by scanning the ads, you would pick up that water filters were something you did not want to sell.

The folks I was consulting with needed a classified ad that would get their phone ringing. In those days, NSA was a machine, and if they got someone in the door, it was a good chance they would join. This was in the late 1980s. Now, their only product was water filters, so they had used the 'Environmental' industry so much that any ad with that in the title or body, would also get 'Is this water filters or is this NSA?' type of questions as soon as the phone was answered, so that was ruled out as well.

What did I do to get the phones ringing off the hook, and build a big leg for these desperate water filter salespeople? Well, I poked around their office looking at their product display. I read the label on one of the filters and noticed that the filter was 'bacteriostatic' – a word I did not know, but I asked about, and learned it meant that bacteria would not grow in the filter. I was told people rarely asked what bacteriostatic meant.

Bingo, I had a brain storm.

My ad:

Earn Over $10,000 per month marketing bacteriostatic units. Retired welcome, call …

That classified ad earned them hundreds of thousands of dollars in sales. Why? Because 99% of people calling on the ad did not know what a 'bacteriostatic unit' was, and were too embarrassed to ask even on the phone. When prospects arrived at the NSA recruiting office, (back then there were hundreds of independent offices for NSA distributors set up as co-ops all over the States, in Canada, and a few in Europe), they would say 'Oh, this is NSA!' but they would usually stay for the presentation, and the NSA folks recruited just as many as usual.

This is the key, find a term no one else is using that is not directly connected to your product, or company, that sounds mysterious, but interesting, but also that few people will ask 'what is that?' for fear of looking uninformed. You will be surprised how few people will ask what something is if they think it will make them look dumb. Lesson here, never, ever be afraid to ask.

Second lesson here: once you have brainstormed and come up with a few different mysterious but intelligent ways to describe your industry or your product you can use it in phone scripts, ads, etc.

Now, typically the receptionist will go and ask the Doctor, and often the Doctor will leave their patient, and ask you a word or two just because this method works so well. Usually, as they are busy, they will come out just to set a time when you can return and presto, you have your meeting.

They may ask you what it's all about, and you say this, while looking at your watch (don't look at a smart phone, look at your watch!), 'Look, it's about nutritional products for the main stream or main stream America – it could be very lucrative, quite a few thousand dollars, but I need someone with a medical degree (who is quite presentable/professional/local/with your background (pick one) – when will you have, say, 30 minutes?'.

If forced to, say 'I'm in events, and seminar productions, and this product is being introduced to the market through some events that I am setting up, but, for more details, I'm afraid we must sit down for 20 minutes or so. When would that be?'. Pull out your diary at that point and look at it. Even if you use a smart phone for your diary, I recommend a paper diary, because it sends a message of making an appointment. If you look at a smart phone, you lose people, as we ignore people who are looking at their phone.

Say nothing else, he or she will set up a time with you, and get back to their patient. This works nearly every time, unless they are afraid of public speaking, and if that is the case, ask them 'Do you know any professionals like yourself that might be perfect as a seminar speaker?' It's rare they don't give you a referral, as Doctors are in the business of making referrals.

Once you have a referral, it's pretty simple to get a meeting with them.

Call the Doctor and speak to receptionist:

'My name is David Williams, Doctor (name of the Doctor who gave you the referral), asked me to call Doctor (name of Doctor you are calling) about being a speaker in a seminar – when can I speak to him/her?'

This will get you a time or a call back from the Doctor.

When you have the Doctor on the phone:

'Thanks for getting back to me Dr. blank, Dr. so-and-so referred you to me about the possibility of us working together on a project. I'm involved in the seminar business, and I'm looking for a professional like yourself to be my main speaker. It can get very lucrative. I don't have a lot of time just this minute, but let me ask you this, are you open to diversifying your income and adding to it?'

Wait for answer, which will be 'yes, but it depends on what it is'.

You: 'Alright, it seems Dr. blank made a good choice in referring you to me, let's set up a 30 minute window to get together, and I'll fill you in. You can decide after that. What's good for you?'

Often they will have the receptionist set up the meeting, or will just say to come over later that day.   In any case, you have a meeting.

Note: sometimes this referral script is just as good as the other scripts above, so test both and see.

Once you have your appointment, you are going to make a 30 minute presentation (or your upline is), about the system.   This is described in a later chapter because I feel it's better you read the book in this order.

Second Chapter: Recruiting Doctors Hidden Source Method

This method works well in big cities, if you don't live in a big city, you can still follow this method if you find a Doctor in your area, or, just pick a city within a 3 hour drive and work the system there.

Did you know there are many more Doctors out there than those who are practicing? There are retired doctors, doctors who don't like to practice, yet have the qualifications, but are not certified in their state or province, but yet they are still Doctors. Some find that they can't work for one reason or another. Some are immigrants, and are qualified in their home country, but not in America, or Canada, or Europe. This is one of the biggest sources of non-practicing Doctors. Often they are driving cabs or working in fast food restaurants. However, they are still Doctors, and can be called such. They can speak about their medical degree, call themselves 'Doctor X' etc. They just can't give any medical advice.

Sometimes they are found in immigrant communities, and this will give you a further opportunity once you have set the system below up, you can do the same thing over again in the language of your Doctor. Sometimes legs in a different culture or language explode in an unexpected way, and grow long distance as well.

How to find these Doctors:

Put in an ad in Craigslist, Backpage.com, or kijiji.ca, and or ebayclassifieds.com seeking non-practicing medical doctors or those who are qualified in other countries, but not here.

Local business person requires a non-practicing Doctor (from any country) for business proposal. Email your contact details for meeting. Could be a very lucrative sideline.

See more samples below. Post as many as you can in different sections of the website, including part time, with different headlines, as per below.

Sample Craigslist ads and headlines:

Are you a Doctor but not certified here?

Unlicensed Doctor?

Medical Degree from outside the US and can't practice here?

Seeking a Doctor from outside the US not practicing here

Uncertified Doctor?

Do you have a Degree in Nutrition(medicine, etc.), or related discipline but are not working in that field?

We are a local business requiring a medical Doctor as a consultant. Very financially rewarding for the right person, all welcome. Email your resume or call...

Also, go to a taxi office, ask 'who is an immigrant doctor driving cab?' there are so many in large cities, you will be amazed. Post up a flyer in their office:

Seeking a Medical Doctor not Practicing in US (or Canada, Europe etc.)

Local business person requires a person with a medical degree as a consultant or more.

Email me at or call

Very financially rewarding for the right person. Could work if you have a background in related areas. Contact me today.

Lastly, look in your yellow pages for 'associations', call each that is regarding another culture and ask if they have any newspapers or websites that take ads, and what local shops have these newspapers for you to look at. Tell them you are seeking a medical Doctor from their community, one that is not yet licensed here. Often they know some-one. Use the newspapers or websites for these communities for your ads to recruit these Doctors as well. Between all these sources, you will find yourself with a good number to pick from. You want the one who will be the best on stage (this will make sense by the time you finish reading this book), if you end up with more than one, you should con-sider sponsoring them under each other, so you have a strong team, and don't have to run different events (again, this will make sense by the time you finish reading this book).

If you have a good hotel in your area, set up your one-on-one meet-ings with your Doctor prospects there, and explain the proposition to your Doctor prospect. Wear a suit and look, act and be professional. Doctors are professionals, and make sure you call your prospect 'Doctor' at each opportunity.

In most cases, this person has not been called 'Doctor' for a while, especially from someone outside his homeland, it will win you respect and gratitude.

As I stated above, you are going to outline the system to your Doctor prospect, the details are in the following chapter, near the end, titled What to say to a Doctor the first time you meet them for your 30 minute presentation.

Now, in the next Chapter, read how this powerful system works.

Third Chapter: How to build your Doctor without warm market!

This is the third part of this secret system: How to build your Doctor's business without warm market – the answer - seminar recruiting.

Note – this is not as simple as doing a Business Opportunity Meeting – BOM. Some parts of this seminar are the same as your BOM, and some general conduct rules apply, but it's very, very different. Pay close attention.

If you leave Doctors to their own devices in MLM, they will fail, or at least have as much chance as anyone else. However, if you follow this recipe for success, you will find yourself with a runaway leg, (in the good sense!).

Just to reiterate, tell your Doctor to forget his warm market, unless he MUST have someone spoken to right now. He's too green to do it himself, but he will have a big ego, and THINK he can. Tell them no, that you and he must follow this plan.

Here is your plan, it's worth millions to you and your Doctor – I have divided it into two parts, and overview, and the details.

Overview:

This plan is predicated on you having a 'Doctor' as your 'main speaker' at a mini-event, or seminar. This 'Doctor' is your draw for you to promote this event. As you read this, you might think 'I could do the speaking myself', that would be true, but you would have missed the point. The point is you need to be the promoter, you need to be the person promoting 'The Doctor' and his message of 'Weight Loss' or

'Extra Energy' – whatever you chose based on what your Wellness product offers best. It could be anti-aging, more strength, etc.

There are two things you are doing; you are setting up a series of mini-seminars (actually, just a presentation by your Doctor), and you are promoting them to local people via gyms, health food stores, yoga centers and related services. Both are key. The major difference between this and a typical BOM is that this seminar is NOT promoted as a 'lead with the opportunity' or making money presentation, instead, its 'product first as presented by a DOCTOR', or a 'Lead with the product' with an 'oh by the way, there is money to be made here' Colombo approach.

Since you are in the Wellness industry, the magic here is having a Doctor to add credibility to your product, because your product is unknown to the people you are promoting it to. Its far easier to pro-mote a seminar with Doctor blank then to promote a seminar about your product. Of course people don't know your Doctor, but they are trained to respect Doctors. Your seminar title is about solving a prob-lem, like weight loss, or increasing our energy, or anti-aging, etc., ac-cording to Dr. blank, this will get more people into the room than to promote 'learn all about Herbalife's amazing shake'. The focus is on a specific benefit, presented by an expert, (your Doctor), and this gets you prospects and bodies on chairs. Your Doctor delivers a good seminar for 30 minutes, people taste/eat/drink or see your product, and then you close the seminar with a short opportunity presentation, but with a major twist: that those in the room are all part of a 'special team' all part of Doctor blank's organization, and they can use this system and the DOCTOR to build their business.

The other factor that makes his work is how you promote this. This is a 'local' meeting, or seminar. You find a local venue, and within a 15 to 20 minute drive of this venue, you are going to promote this health seminar to people interested in your topic, by promoting it in gyms, health food shops, yoga studios, etc., etc. The 'how to' details are contained below. Now it's time for the details!

The Details:

Get your hands on a PowerPoint presentation on your company's products. You will need to make some changes. You will need Microsoft PowerPoint, or the comparable free product by Open office called Impress, http://www.openoffice.org/download/index.html or you can use Google's own free version called Presentations. These are free. Apple has keynote.

You will create your own version of your company product presentation, but you will do it a bit differently.

Rather than the typical structure of a BOM, (company, products and compensation plan, close, break, training or second close), you are going to have this as your plan:

Intro – You

Problem – The Doctor

Solution – The Doctor

Try – Taste – the Product (the solution) – The Doctor or You

Close on Products – You until your Doctor can

Break

Mini Compensation Plan – You

Close – You

Let's break each down:

Problem – there are two different meetings you can typically do for a nutritional product, Weight Loss, or Increased Energy. Both are different, so it's best to do two different events, and not mix the two subjects It will give you much more room for growth by doing two different events.

So, depending on which one of the two you are presenting that night, you need some slides with some quotes about the challenges of either. Google is your friend, you can get great info online to build up 3 slides ONLY on this subject of your 'Problem'. You can get free royalty free pictures for slides by searching Google images, settings, and select Advanced Image Search, usage rights, free to use or share. As long as you don't charge anyone to get in the door, you are ok, as it's not a commercial seminar. You can do a co-op for expenses, i.e. it's a not-for-profit event in the future, but at this point is does not matter. This is a free seminar by a health professional.

Solution – offer some solutions – come up with some difficult solutions that are unpractical – like weight loss by jogging 90 minutes per day, or bulking up in the gym, the presenter will make some jokes about these 'solutions', that it's not easy, etc. 'These are not practical solutions for most of us, as we are too busy 'caring for kids, busy at work, being a Doctor, anyone with an injury can't jog etc, etc'.

'Therefore, we need an edge.'

The edge of course, is … your product. No doubt this will be easy to write since most of your BOM will have parts of this in it, your job is to make the Seminar into a 'Problem – Solution' format. At this point you can use your normal product slides, but only offer the point where you bring in the products that solve the problem. You don't want your company name mentioned until you are in the solution stage, and only because you are now talking about the product. It's very important to state again – your product as a solution is the key, not the company, how old it is, or who founded it, etc. etc., they will learn all of that when they join up and go to an average BOM.

NB: Even if your company has a skin care line, now is not the time to mix messages by bringing it up. Your future distributors will find out later, and that's fine.

Your slides should include pictures with lots of product success stories.

Arrange to have your Doctor meet those in your company who have great product stories. Using your carfare, take pictures of your Doctor and those with good product testimonials. This is easy to do at a local meetings. Or, if a regional conference or training is going on you can find many people there happy to have their picture taken with a Doctor. Product stories are very good.

Remember: Facts Tell, Stories Sell.

Just to cover yourself, and especially if your Doctor is not certified to practice, a good idea is to have a disclaimer slide up under the welcome, and during your intro. Most people are used to hearing medical disclaimers on ads, and understand the law is complex and that a disclaimer is a standard policy.

The following disclaimer was taken and adapted from http://www.freenetlaw.com/templates/medical-disclaimer-template.php

MEDICAL DISCLAIMER

No advice

This presentation contains general information about medical conditions and treatments. The information is not advice, and should not be treated as such.

Limitation of warranties

The medical information on this presentation is provided "as is" without any representations or warranties, express or implied. [NAME] makes no representations or warranties in relation to the medical information in this presentation.

Without prejudice to the generality of the foregoing paragraph, [NAME] does not warrant that:

the medical information in this presentation is complete, true, accurate, up-to-date, or non-misleading.

Professional assistance

You must not rely on the information in this presentation as an alternative to medical advice from your doctor or other professional healthcare provider.

If you have any specific questions about any medical matter you should consult your doctor or other professional healthcare provider.

If you think you may be suffering from any medical condition you should seek immediate medical attention.

You should never delay seeking medical advice, disregard medical advice, or discontinue medical treatment because of information on this website.

Liability

Nothing in this medical disclaimer will limit any of our liabilities in any way that is not permitted under applicable law, or exclude any of our liabilities that may not be excluded under applicable law.

Don't let it scare anyone, I would usually joke about the fine print, and warn people that 'Caution, McDonald's Coffee is Hot'.

This whole event should not take longer than one hour, but that can take practice. You will have people hanging around joining for longer than an hour, but you don't want them sitting in chairs for more than forty-five minutes listening to your or your Doctor.

Remember – the brain can absorb only what the bum can endure.

Have your Doctor learn the presentation. Have him read all the product info from the company, and anything else they can on the products. Add photos you took of the Doctor and those with great product stories into the PowerPoint presentation. You need to link your Doctor to these stories and images are a great way to do this. Look for stories about weight loss, increased energy, etc., things that can appeal to the masses, not things that are only going to appeal to a small number of people like a weird illness.

You Doctor has to know that you and he will be working these events for the next 90 days.

Now, while your Doctor is learning his product presentation, you are promoting the local 'event'.

First, locate a suitable venue. It could be a school after hours, a meeting room in a gym, in a hotel, but it must be 'local' to the area you are in. You can do many different areas, but learn the system first before you branch out too much.

Once you have your venue, you create some flyers. You will be going to local gyms and health food stores, and will pass out these flyers. Make friends with the staff, bring them coffees or teas. You will be surprised what people will do for a free coffee now an then.

I used to send flyers to companies that had employee mail boxes, (even today in age of emails, so many companies still use paper). I would send a box of flyers about an upcoming presentation, and include either a lottery ticket or a one of those large chocolate bars as a gift to the head of the mail room. This was not for a nutritional event, as you could have guessed, but these folks would put my flyers into the employee mail boxes every two weeks, for a $5 lottery ticket, or big chocolate bar! These days, dollar stores have lots of items that make good gifts. People will actually do more for you if you give them a lower value bribe than if you give them a big bribe.

You just want to make sure they give your flyers out. If they won't, stand outside the gym and pass out flyers. This is your job until you have a downline. Do it all day for a couple of weeks, at different local gyms. Engage people, don't act like you are just paid to pass out flyers. The more personal your contact with someone is, the more the odds they will come. If you are at the gym often and they see you, it's also more likely they attend. If they see you a minimum of 3 times you are doing a basic job, seven times, you are a super star and you are on your way to wealth. Remember, after a few events, you will have downline to take over. Buy a sandwich for the gym manager. He or she will see you hanging around and a quick word about what you are doing will get them on side, as will the sandwich.

While you are out there doing this, alone and wondering if it's all worth it, remember all of these folks will be in your team, so suck it up and get out there. Let the rest buy leads and become broke telemarketers.

As you hand out your flyers, speak about this great free seminar. Promote, promote, and promote! Put your flyers on the windows of cars parked near the gym. Hit yoga studios, and any place where people who want to be fit and healthy go. Diet places like Weight Watchers is another example. Using Google, look up all the gyms, health food shops, natural healers, etc. in your areas, i.e. the area close to your venue. Don't do the other side of town, this is a local meeting, you are focusing on one area at a time.

You can create a good flyer with Microsoft Word, or any other comparable product. You can find templates on the web for flyers, you can even search for 'health flyer' and get ideas. Pick a topic: Weight loss, or Increased Energy. Your flyer will say the date, time and address of the event, and say something like this:

Monday, 7:30 PM ONLY!

The Secrets of Increased Energy

With Dr. – fill in your Doctor's name

Learn how to get up to 1000% of an energy increase without drugs, exercise, yoga, chanting, or any other crazy idea. (you many change and edit this, this is only an example)

Dr. blank will reveal to you a substance that will change your energy and life forever! Less than the price of a cup of coffee, and far more powerful, without any weird side effects.

Free Sample!!! (only 1 per person so bring your spouse!)

Don't miss your chance to have more Energy!

Monday, 7:30 ONLY

St. Peters High School, North Entrance, Free Parking

Optional is to put a phone number – I like to use a local Voice Mail number if you can find one. Put a 60 second pitch with the info in it.

Thanks for calling the Energy Seminar (local neighborhood name) information line. Yes, the Energy (or weight loss) seminar is being held at St. Peters High School on Monday, the 12th of May. Bring your spouse as there will be only one free product per person, and you're both going to want to experience the difference. Our guest speaker is Dr. blank, who is an expert on how this incredible product can help you sleep better, feel much more energetic, eliminate mental fog, perform better at the gym, etc. etc. (list benefits of your product in relation to the type of event you are offering but not its name!!!). Please arrive five minutes early!

You will repeat this system in as many local areas as you have in your city, if you live in a big city, you will never finish. You will be rich.

The Event:

Best case scenario is the following set up, if you can't afford some of the tools, do your best.

Have someone outside the door, at a table, with a sign in form. Get the name and mobile number (which is good for texting the next meet info), and for following up. You can also have a spot for home phone and email, few will fill in all of that, but try at least to get a mobile number. Keep records and follow up on all your attendees.

You will need your laptop and a projector for your PowerPoint slides, often a venue has a screen for projecting on, or if not, take a look in advance – many walls offer just as good a surface to project on these days. Try it out and see. If you need a screen, you can also use white bristle board found in dollar stores.

See if you can control the lights from inside the room, or not. If you can't turn them off, and your projector is not bright enough to project well in a room lightly lit, you will need a different venue. Some places the lights on or off is all or nothing, pitching your room into total darkness save for the projector is also not a good idea. If that is the case bring lamp or two for the table at the back of the room.

You can rent a projector, or buy one. Their prices are very low these days, and you can get a good deal at www.tigerdirect.com. You will need a laptop, and some of you may even know how to use a iPad or tablet with a projector. If you don't know anything about these items, they are very easy to learn, and are not hard to find. For a lower price alternative, make your PowerPoint slides, save them to a disk and take the disk to Staples to have your sides printed out on transparencies. You will need to get a used overhead projector, or borrow one. It's pretty '80's but it will work, and you should be able to get one cheap. If your Doctor is a working or practicing Doctor, they may have connections to equipment like this.

I suggest you contact an upline to see who has a projector, if you hold your events on days that don't conflict with a BOM, you may get some assistance.

NOTE: You don't want your upline to spread the word about your event or you will find problems. You need to assure the Doctor that all the people in the room will be part of his team, not just to make him feel good, but because the system depends on you being able to tell every-one in the room they are part of this marketing system. If you have some folks you can trust to come and help you, like family members of the Doctor or yourself, that will be a big help to work the door, passing out product, etc. It won't be for long, because once you sign up a few people, you can have them take over the job on the door, or passing out material, product etc.

Remember: You will have to be careful when or if you tell your up-line, as you will have to explain it's not an open meeting. He or she will want it to be, 'we are all one family' etc., (his family) but you must be strong and say no. It's just the way it is. Your upline should be happy someone has the initiative to do this, and you only need his or her help a few times, until you have enough bodies recruited to help out. If it was me, I would skip using an upline unless I was a total newbie.

Depending on the room, you will need to use a microphone and speaker system to be sure everyone can hear you. It's not just because your voice needs to reach the back of the room, it's also much more professional, and, if your Doctor has an accent, or comes from some culture where they are not strong or loud speakers, a microphone and speaker system is a must. Lots of this hardware can be found by going online to craigslist etc., or ebay. Craigslist will allow you to see it and try it out before you buy, as the seller is local. I like having my own equipment, as then I am in control of it. It's a business expense, and you will eventually have a co-op and charge your team members a nominal monthly fee to offset these costs, and this includes your outlay.

For an inexpensive alternative try a karaoke machine. I like the small tie clip microphones, with very long extension wires while some people like to hold a mic, either is fine. The radio microphones are good, but can screw up. That's why I prefer a wired mic, with a long extension cord so you can walk around. You can get these at The Source. Some venues are so small you will not need any, like boardrooms, but the idea is to have a seminar with 30 plus people, and if you build for this event properly and promote it locally as per this book, you may have standing room only. Board room events are something you will grow out of very quickly.

Speaking of standing room only, have less chairs out than you expect to need. Before the meeting, stack up lots of the chairs at the back of the room. As people come in, have the back row of chairs 'reserved' with random business cards or tape. People always take the last row, which leaves the front row empty. As you need new seats, just take out a few at a time, after you have 'unsaved' the back row. It needs to look like you were unprepared for so many people. You want people to be thinking 'wow, they did not expect so many people, I'm glad I came, it must be pretty good'.

Dress for success. Suits for you and your Doctor if male, or power outfit for female. If you have any help from family or friends, once again, suit and tie. It makes a difference.

Get an old fashioned boom box for music, or, if you have your speaker system, just lay your mic beside your laptop speaker and play some music, your live mic will send the sound through the sound system. You can even Google 'best music for MLM' for ideas.

Make sure you have the music playing before the event starts, before anyone sets foot through the door, so they hear it from the hallway. Make sure the music is fast, upbeat, and loud. You need to have it loud enough that people need to shout to speak, NOT like being in a church, but like a party. Its better they don't or can't talk and must shout to each other rather than just sit on their chairs in silence thinking of where they could be while they wait for you to start. If someone asks you to turn down the music say 'we're working on it', and thank them.

Just a note, if you like classical music, or country, etc., forget about it. Play fast music, with a rapid beat. It will get the heart pumping and put people into an excited mood. It's not about you, it's about the event.

Start on time, or at worst 3 minutes late. Don't hold back hoping for stragglers. You do the presentation for those who came, and not for those who did not. If you have been promoting it, you will have people arriving. Don't let people see you looking at the door, expectantly. Teach your people that too.

Don't have any company material visible, posters, etc., you don't anyone to make any premature decisions, 'Oh, my uncle Tony was in this, and he said...'

Have your PowerPoint slides up with a welcome page, (again, no company logos etc.). Once your room is full, you shut the door, and have someone turn off the music as your run up to the stage or front of the room, and welcome everyone. If the music is loud enough, turning it off suddenly will signal everyone something is happening.

Thank everyone for coming, and welcome them to hear this Energy Seminar or Weight Loss Seminar, whichever one you have on that night. Introduce yourself, and tell your product story, without giving the name of the product, just say 'the product that we are introducing to you tonight', and how it has helped you. Now you introduce the next and main speaker by giving his background, why he is there, and lastly, his name, his name is the last thing you say, and say it loud. That is his clue to run up on stage and thank you. If you have any people in the crowd that are part of your team, or family members, this is also the clue to clap. Clapping is good for everyone. This is your last line: Now, I'd like to bring up our main speaker, someone who is an expert in blank – DOCTOR PETER YORK!!! Or, Please help me welcome DOCTOR PETER YORK!!! If you say it right, people know when to clap. Make the last word you say the loudest. If you clap too, it sends the same message.

If your Doctor has a very difficult last name, drop it and use his first name only. 'Doctor Raj'. If neither are easy anglicize it. This book is not meant to be politically correct advice, just good advice. Use it or not.

Your Doctor now takes over, and does his product slides. Don't worry, he will get better and better. He does not speak about the business, or hint at it. If you have some people to do product testimonials, he can bring them up at the right time, near the end of his presentation.

Once he has concluded, he turns the meeting back over to you, by asking you to come up.

You run up and say, smiling, 'wow, wasn't that fantastic, (as you are clapping), let's give Doctor Peter a big round – or another big round'. Clapping is good, it's very positive and actually makes people feel good. Don't skip these little things.

In the meantime, you have set up the back of the room with juice samples, (or whatever product you sell), so it's time to pass them out on trays. If you don't have people to pass out the samples, ask two people from the audience to do it. Yes, that's what I wrote. I have gotten prospects to work the door, introduce me and even make name tags in my day. People are willing and happy to help if you ask them nicely.

You tell the audience they can purchase the product here now, and when you break in just a few minutes, they can just go to the back of the room to pick up their own. You will sell some so have some on hand. It looks weak if you say 'well, we have to order in some', it looks as if you did not expect to sell any. If your Doctor has funds, a good way to get him or her to place a big order is to explain all the sales in the room are his, and he gets the money right back and that order may move him up in your structure. However, this is not the reason for having him or her, if they are broke and willing and able, don't force the issue of buying product. The presentations they do is worth the effort, not the single order you can get from your Doctor. It's the name 'Doctor' gets the bodies in seats.

If you can't afford to pre-order product yourself or through your Doctor, ask around from your upline or sideline, making sure you can bring back what you can't sell, and order more yourself to replace what you do sell. Don't give your upline or sideline the cash, or you will not get credit for promotion for your sales. Your Doctor needs to see this product volume go under his distributorship position. Have people there to help you pass out product samples and take orders. Your Doctor could have their wife/husband, kids etc. there too.

How do you bring up the MLM side of your business in your Energy or Weight Loss seminar?

Simple: You mention that anyone here tonight can buy these products retail or wholesale. 'Hands up who would rather pay a wholesale price?' NOTE: any time you ask for a show of hands, raise your own hand. People do what they see, and if you raise your hand, (slowly but firmly and high), it will send them 'permission' to do the same.

'Why wholesale? Well, we have a problem, our problem is the fact that everyone needs this product and we don't have enough people to market it. We like to market through seminars, like this, with Dr. blank as the speaker. If you would like to stay after the break to learn how to make a lucrative income, please do.'

Now hand out a copy of some great stories of those from your company that have had success with the products on one side of the handout, and the opportunity on the other. Have your phone number and the Doctor's on this sheet. This should be only one page, double-sided, not a flashy folder of material, (only put the first name of the person in the story). This is just an 8.5 x 11 inch print out on yellow or canary colored paper. Staple your business card to it, or the Doctor's.

After the break YOU do a mini opportunity presentation, without having to cover the products. Explain that this is network marketing, but how much easier it is, because everyone here tonight has Dr. blank as his sponsor or upline, ('hands up – how many here tonight think it would be much easier to sponsor someone if they had Doctor blank to help them do the recruiting?') and that you do this business unlike any other person in MLM, you do it through seminars, and offer to share with them this system, (not the whole thing, but the part where they can pass out flyers in gyms, etc., all over the city and have the Doctor work his magic).

Now, if you want, you can add 'this is NOT your typical MLM forcing you to go after your warm market, that is old school MLM – this is seminar marketing – with a health professional at the helm, and the key is Product First – it's not Opportunity Driven'. This appeals to some people.

Eventually you will phase your people into the open BOM's of your company, so they can use them as a tool as well. They will have two types of meetings, yours and the company BOMs. Twice the chance of success.

'This will build big and fast, if there is anyone you know personally that they would like our help to sponsor, (you and the Doctor), get them here next week, especially if they have had some experience in MLM. This way, once you start sponsoring strangers, you can put those strangers in your friends team, thus helping them'. This will usually will get you a couple of people in that new team, because these people know that they will be sponsoring strangers under their friends, (I hate to say 'under someone', but it makes it easier to understand).   This is sometimes called the 'Big Al' technique.

Following up:

Advise your Doctor to get a separate number for this business, if they have a busy practice. You can get a phone number from Google, or other company online, but make sure it's a local area code. Have the Doctor share that Voice Mail password with you.

You do the call backs, and just start off each call back conversation and follow up call with 'Doctor blank asked me to call you back, as he's busy today in the operating room/saving lives/flying Airforce One, (just checking to see if you are awake) or something that sounds real without lying. It's better that you do the close as its 'business' and your Doctor is too green at this point.

'Can you see how doing MLM this way, with a Doctor at the helm, as your upline, makes building a business much easier?'

'Can you see yourself succeeding having this type of system to build your business with?'

What to say to a Doctor the first time you meet them for your 30 minute presentation

As I stated prior, if your Doctor does not have a practice or an office, meet them in a nice hotel lobby for the one-on-one meeting. This will give you some class by association. Many non-MLM business meetings are done this way, and often you can have a coffee served to you. Lots of hotels have free Internet access should you need it, but otherwise the staff won't bother you. If your Doctor has a practice, usually you will meet at their office, which is fine.

Generally, you are going to show the Doctor the 'short' version of your company business presentation. However, before you do, you are going to frame it differently. Framing is everything. Context is another word for framing.

This is the context or frame for your meeting:

Tell them you are an MLM professional, ('yes, don't roll your eyes yet, I'm not here to sponsor you into my business and have phoning your friends or any of your patients. I'm here about a seminar marketing position and it won't take me too much time to show it to you – and if I didn't think you could earn $(big amount) I wouldn't be here wasting either of our time. Just bear with me for ten minutes).

Now, many of the 'new American' immigrant Doctors don't know about MLM or they are not that negative about it, so you may not get the 'social stigma' objection that a practicing Doctor will have, so you will not have to use the above to get past that objection. Lastly, remind the practicing Doctor that, 'while you may have heard many things about MLM or Network Marketing, both pro and con, one thing you have heard is the fact that many people make a few hundred thousand dollars per month doing it, but those that do, follow a unique system, something 90% of people never see, but I'm going to show you today', (that should shut them up and give you their attention).

If the Doctor is an immigrant, test him on his knowledge of MLM, be sure they understand the concept, if they don't, just explain to them your normal or standard business presentation, with him or her as the product presenter in seminars. You can be very straight forward with them, as they are usually very open and flattered to be important again.

If the new immigrant Doctor knows about MLM, (chances are some-one tried to sponsor them into something by now), you will get the objection that they don't know anyone, never made money, etc. The real point is they don't think they can make money, and don't know anyone here.   You point out you don't want them talking to anyone except those you put in front of them, in a seminar format. That they don't need to know anyone, you are going to find the people.

Now, outline the system to them, playing on their vanity, and see how many of them agree. You can build up one team per city, or per local area, putting each of them under the most promising Doctor you find, or you can sponsor each of them direct to you. If you build a team - all under one Doctor- its stronger and they can depend on each other. If you repeat this in different cities and areas, you will leave a stronger team that does not need you faster and thus, you have duplicated yourself quicker.

Going back to the Doctor with a practice, now that you have framed your presentation, you explain the system that you have planned. That you, as the upline, will do all the heavy lifting, organizing the venue, finding the prospects, and setting up the event. All your Doctor must do is practice the presentation, and deliver it. You would like them to see a standard BOM just to get the feel of the company, products etc., but they are to under no circumstances reveal to anyone your system. Now is the time to show them some pictures or videos of Doctor's in your program making a lot of money. You can also show them Doctors making big money in other programs, (don't worry, they won't remem-ber the names). Your point is that DOCTORS make the big money, and they are Doctors.   Show big money when you show your compensation system, and explain its realistic because you are filling rooms, and the people in the room are all part of the Doctors pay line.

Sometimes you can use a Non-Disclosure Agreement with your Doctor prior to starting the presentation, which gives you a bit of an edge, as people value something that is secret from others more than something that is not. The fact that you also don't want them talking to family or anyone else will make them take you more seriously, and believe in your plan. No doubt the last person who tried to interest them in a MLM venture said, 'wow, with all your contacts from medical school, ex-patients, current patients, and everyone in the hospital, you could reach Double Gold Diamond Crown Vice President Ambassador Director in no time and be pinned at our Homecoming next year!'

Your main point is that YOU are serious, can deliver prospects in the seminar, and YOU can do the follow ups, all your Doctor must do is show up and deliver a good seminar.

Perhaps I should reassure you at this point, that once the Doctor sees this plan working, they will want to take it over, and let them, as soon as you feel they can. Typically, you will find some of the new people in their team to take over your roll, as they want to build and recruit in the gym etc.

For practicing Doctors, you may have to pitch 10 to find one, for immigrant or non-practicing Doctors, its far less. Both have pros and cons, but either way, like any kind of recruiting, you never stop building.

Conclusion

At this point, I think you can see how this system works, you just keep doing it over and over. Eventually your Doctor gets the idea and will find other Doctors who can speak to groups. They are over the 'friends and family' excuse because they see it as seminar marketing, something that Doctors are used to due to attending conferences where drug sellers make presentations all the time.

I have revealed enough information for you to do this on your own. If you have any experience doing meetings you will be far ahead, or you can find an upline who can help.

This system can be worked over and over again. That's one of its big advantages, even every two months in the same area. You don't need the internet, or a large budget, or a lot of experience. Just get busy and get rich - with Doctors!

Contact me at DavidWilliamsAuthor@gmail.com anytime.

A note about one of my other books:

The Simplest, Shortest, Most Powerful MLM and Network Marketing Prospect Control and Closing Lines and Scripts - it's a .99 cent marvel!

By David Williams

http://www.amazon.com/Simplest-Shortest-Powerful-Marketing-ebook/dp/B00BW7KJ38/ref=pd_rhf_dp_p_t_2_16S2

Do you have trouble closing prospects? Do you feel you lose control of your prospecting and follow up calls? Do you have trouble closing strong prospects – the very ones you desperately want on your team?

Well, this book is for you. It's the lowest price but highest value book on Amazon. Why? Because this little book contains over 120 of the strongest, easiest, subtlest closing and 'keeping control' and 'taking control' over the conversation lines for network marketers.

FULL DISCLOSURE: This is a short book. This book has over 150 'lines'; mostly one line sentences. But don't be fooled by the size of the book. These are powerful closing lines to allow you to close your pro-spect. This is NOT a book on prospecting, recruiting or even a script book.

This is a book that should be open at your desk as you make your prospecting and follow up calls. If you find you prospect off their script (they never stay on script – only you can do that), these lines will bring you back into control.

They are subtle, but powerful. Here's some samples:

How much does it cost?

Millions of dollars not to get involved

Can you see yourself taking people through a process just like I did with you?

You can't outsource your learning

The table's set

This is thick

I'm not claiming we have an automatic system, I'm demonstrating it

Get into the game with us

Let me layout how the business will start for you

This is just a process to see if there a fit for you

This is not a pressure gig

It's just the way we do this (process)

There's no glory in paying bills

I promise I'm not going to push you, chase you or sell you

I'm not going to come back to close you, but to personalize the business for you

NOTE: with very little modification, you can use many of these lines as ad headers, email subject lines, or as smart and directed text in emails or create new phone scripts or reinvigorate old ones.

Now, you don't have to memorize these lines, you just need to have your Kindle reader, iPad or even your Kindle for PC open, (or you can print out the pages), when you are making your calls. If you lose control of a conversation, or have a strong person on the line (the best kind to recruit), these 'lines' are the arrows in your quiver.

Make these lines your own. They have been collected by professionals and have earned those who have used them millions of dollars, no exaggerating, millions of dollars. Now for .99 cents they are yours.

This book of powerful network marketing closing and control lines provides you with the easiest way to sound strong on the phone. You just need to use them. You need to sound strong. Your prospect will never know what hit them until you are training them, and tell them to pick up this little book.

If they won't spend .99 cents, to get a copy, they aren't worth your time. If they ask you to make them a copy instead, they have just told you they are not worth your time. You now own this book, make these lines your own, become powerful and rich.

You do deserve it!

http://www.amazon.com/Simplest-Shortest-Powerful-Marketing-ebook/dp/B00BW7KJ38/ref=pd_rhf_dp_p_t_2_16S2

Here are two other books by different authors I would like to plug:

They are about two different nutritional MLM companies, each of which work will with the system for recruiting Doctors very well. Both of these books are perfect 'third party verification' books, great for lending (the hard copy) or showing the Kindle copy to prospects. What I like about both books is that the authors allow you to send to them your product story, which he will include in updated editions, (which are fast for Kindle books, and even for the hard copy editions since they are printed on demand). If you are in Zija or MonaVie, you should order both a Kindle copy and a Hard copy, and you should give the book a review on Amazon AND include your product story in the review with your real name in the review. Eventually your prospects will see it, and be impressed.

What is MonaVie? What is Acai Berry? Miracle or Sham? A Business Analysis and MonaVie Review by Kevin Lindsey

Kindle Edition:

http://www.amazon.com/MonaVie-Miracle-Business-Analysis-ebook/dp/B00BWDNR72

Hard copy edition:

http://www.amazon.com/What-MonaVie-Acai-Berry-Miracle/dp/1483909794

and

What is Zija? What is in Zija? What is Moringa? A Business and Health Singularity by Max Hailey

Kindle edition:

http://www.amazon.com/Moringa-Business-Health-Singularity-ebook/dp/B00BYIZ3GI

Hard copy edition:

http://www.amazon.com/What-Zija-Moringa-Business-Singularity/dp/1483939820

Lastly, if you liked my book, (and not the grammar), please do me the kindness of leaving a review on Amazon. You know the value of promotion, and I know you will have found this book very intriguing to say the least. Best of success with YOUR business, David Williams

Contact me at DavidWilliamsAuthor@gmail.com anytime.

Made in the USA
San Bernardino, CA
22 March 2014